Napkins

Little Tricks that Make a Big Impression

> Author: Caroline Hofman | Photos: Manfred Jahreiß | Eva Wunderlich

Contents

Theory

Instructions

Appendix

Effective Napkins — Quick and Easy

Creative napkins set the tone and enhance any table setting. This book offers fresh ideas on napkin design that are quick and easy to implement and sure to inspire you, even if you've never exactly been an "artiste." And best of all, almost everything can be found around any house or garden. Surprise your guests again and again with new napkin ideas, from conservative to colorful, from classic to sophisticated. It's a beautiful way to visually highlight any festive meal.

What You Need

1 | Basic equipment

There are a few basic things you should have on hand for crafts and napkin design. Here's a list of the most important ones. You'll find additional materials and tools on subsequent pages.

• Cardboard (any shapes and colors)
• Fabric scraps (any colors and materials)
• Wire
• Scissors for paper
• Retractable knife (3/8 in with replaceable blades)
• Set square or ruler (preferably metal for using with the knife)

• Wide and fine synthetic brushes (synthetic bristles are easier to clean, are solvent-resistant, keep their shape, and are generally more elastic and durable)
• Adhesive (for information on the best for each situation, see page 6)

2 | Cloth napkins

Cloth napkins give your table a stylish, sophisticated appearance. Beautiful napkins, perhaps with fancy napkin rings, are an essential component of special meals. Cloth napkins are also the most suitable for folding. They are available in all colors and materials, and they're also relatively quick and easy to make yourself if you have a sewing machine. Store-bought cloth napkins are also easy to dye (you'll find suitable cloth products in the housewares department in department stores and drug stores).

2 *Both cloth and paper napkins lend themselves to creative designs.*

You can further enhance cloth napkins by painting or embroidering them or applying some of the creative ideas in this book. Then fold, decorate, or package them.

3 | Paper napkins

These are available in almost any color and with printed designs for every possible occasion. They're an economical and cheerful alternative to cloth napkins. Paper napkins are also great for creative designs. Because they aren't washable, you naturally expect to use them only once. This means you're free to create without having to worry about whether colors and adhesives can be washed out.

1 *You're sure to succeed with the right "tools."*

Materials

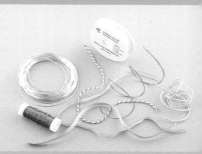

aper

ne following types of paper
vailable at art supply or craft
ores) are used frequently in
is book:

Brown craft wrapping paper
rom a roll)
Japanese (or origami)
Translucent vellum
Gift wrap
Wallpaper scraps
Newspaper and magazine
ippings for paper fringes
nd collages
Gold and silver foil paper
Victorian scraps
Parchment craft paper (lightest
eight you can find)
Tissue paper (colored on both
des, 20 x 28 in)

Felt

Felt is elastic, very easy to cut,
punch holes in, sew, stretch,
baste and glue, and the cut
edges don't fray or fuzz. Felt is
available in a wide range of
colors, precut or on rolls. Craft
felt isn't washable, but natural
and wool felts are washable.

As mentioned above, felt cannot
only be sewn, but can also be
glued. Suitable adhesives
include transfer glue, double-
sided tape, contact adhesive,
and spray adhesive.

Ribbons, etc.

Gift wrapping ribbon is a fast and
economical way to enhance any
creative design. You'll find it in all
craft stores, stationery stores, or
even department stores in every
imaginable form. Most gift ribbon
is washable. The following can
also be used for winding around,
threading, and tying:
• Twine made from natural fibers
• String on a roll
• Flower wire (available in many
colors and thickness)
• Silver wire (for stringing
beads, fastening, and winding
around objects)
• Colored string
• Transparent nylon thread
(in different thickness)

Materials

Adhesives

Universal adhesives (e.g., UHU or Elmer's) are best for paper and cardboard because they dry without warping.

Photo glue (e.g., rubber cement) should always be used when you want to unstick the materials afterward without leaving any residue behind.

Spray adhesives are especially good for gluing large areas without air pockets, but also when you want to attach small decorations such as glitter.

Tempera paints

These are available in almost every color, they cover well and can be thinned with water and are fade-resistant. Tempera paint is applied to grease-free surfaces with a paintbrush. It is suitable for different materials including paper, cardboard, glass, stone, and wood.

The colors are easy to mix. By adding a little white, you can produce beautiful pastel-colored gradations.

Paint markers

These are special pens that cover like paint, have a round tip, and are permanent and water-resistant. They're best for use on vellum paper and plastic film. Paint markers are available from many manufacturers and in many versions.

eads

ou'll find these in craft and bead
ores. They're available in a
riety of colors that are easy
 combine. It's best to string
eads on a nylon thread, but
ote the different hole sizes
hen selecting the beads.

equins are a variation on beads.
hey're available in packages of
e or many colors and provide
 attractive backing for small
ass beads.

Aluminum foil designs

These are creative decorating
items that you can put together
in a flash. They can be bent into
any shape and made to suit all
occasions. All you need is a
standard roll of aluminum foil.
Take a foil strip, squeeze it
together, and twist it into a sort of
cord. You can then shape this cord
into ornaments, figures, or letters.
It's also easy to attach different
figures together simply by
twisting together the lower ends.

Odds and ends

Nifty objects like plastic flowers,
aluminum letters, or tiny mirrors
are a quick and economical way
to enliven any design and really
take your guests by surprise.
You'll find such objects in home
decorating, craft, and toy stores.

A nice variation is to use objects
you find around your house. Every
household has discarded toys,
old souvenirs, etc., that can be
made into funny, clever attention-
grabbers. You can combine
almost anything—let your
imagination run wild!

Materials

Twigs and flowers

These add a touch of nature and freshness to your table. They lend a sophisticated and tranquil stylishness, often accompanied by interesting scents. Twigs and flowers can be placed alongside, inserted in or laid on top of napkins. You can also thread flowers onto rings or strings. But be sure to cut and arrange fresh flowers and herbs at the last possible moment, i.e. just before your guests arrive, so they'll stay fresh for as long as possible.

Scents

The natural scents of flowers and herbs are wonderful "decorations" that add another dimension to napkin creation. Many herbs are also beautiful, which means they can easily be integrated into your table decorations. You can use dried or fresh herbs, from your own garden or from the windowsill. Some of the more expressive include lavender, rosemary, thyme, basil, and marjoram. Other decorating favorites are sage, star anise, cloves, fennel seeds, aniseed, caraway seeds, and dried ginger.

Asian accents

A visit to an Asian market is always inspiring for napkin creation. On the one hand, Asian cuisine is a rich source of unusual and visually enchanting foods such as dried seaweed, sesame crackers, fortune cookies, dried lychees, candied lotus root, colorful rice crackers, bread rings, dried red melon seeds, etc. At the same time, Asian shops carry many everyday objects that can be beautifully integrated into napkin creations, such as chopsticks, incense sticks, and different types of Japanese paper.

Techniques

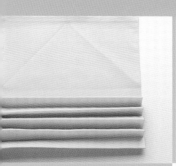

roning

he most important technique
n napkin folding is ironing. You
vant your creations to hold their
hape and not immediately
ollapse in a heap. First iron the
apkin flat. Starch will give it the
ecessary rigidity so the creases
nd folds will maintain their
hape. Each time you make
nother fold, iron it flat again.
nother technique sometimes
sed is to press the folded napkin
etween heavy books.

Laminating

You can take interesting paper
packaging, photos, postcards,
newspaper clippings, or collages
to any copy shop to be laminated,
i.e. sealed in a transparent plastic
film. This will enhance the look
of your decorations as well as
preserve and protect them.

Laminating film comes in different
thickness and in letter- and
ledger/tabloid-sized formats. If
you want to make the laminated
object into a napkin pocket, use
the thinnest film. The two thicker
kinds are good for making ledger-
sized placemats.

Eyelets

Eyelets are a simple but
sophisticated way to bind
together different materials. You
can buy eyelets and eyelet pliers
at hardware stores and at many
fabric stores.

Eyelets are available in many
colors and sizes (in this book,
we use eyelets with a $^3/_{16}$ in
diameter). You can buy them in
complete sets comprising 50
eyelets and a simple pair of eyelet
pliers, which is more than enough
for most crafts. If you develop a
taste for this technique and end
up using your eyelet pliers more
often, you might want to purchase
a high-quality pair with greater
leverage that requires less force.
Here's how it's done: Punch a hole
in the appropriate spot, set the
eyelet into the hole, squeeze it
together, and you're done!

Classic Napkin Folding

A folded cloth napkin is a classic that never goes out of style. These napkins are the true stars of any table decoration, owing mainly to their bright colors and astonishing shapes. See for yourself—there's nothing old-fashioned about them!

Easy

Cigar

➤ 1 cloth napkin,
20 x 20 in

1 band, 2³/₄ x 8 in
(use gift-wrapping or
brown-wrapping paper)

Japanese paper,
1¹/₂ x 1¹/₂ in

1
*Fold over the top and
bottom edges of the napkin
inward to meet at the
middle. From the center
point, fold the four corners
outward on an angle.*

2
*Start from the right side, and roll
up the napkin. Do the same from
the left side so that the two rolls
meet in the center.*

3
*Place the band around
the two cigars. Glue the
Japanese paper square
onto the band.*

Advanced | Festive

Lily

➤ 1 cloth napkin, 20 x 20 in

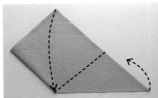

1 *Fold the napkin in half diagonally with the open end pointed upward. Fold the two outer corners inward to meet at the top. Then fold the two tips of these corners back downward to the bottom corner.*

2 *Fold the upper corner down so it overlaps the center line by about 2 1/2 in.*

3 *Fold the tip of this corner back underneath the napkin.*

4 *Fold the upper section down at the center line.*

5 *Turn the napkin over and tuck the two corners into one another so they are secured.*

6 *Turn napkin back over, stand it up and pull down on the two tips of the outer layer of cloth.*

Easy

Four Corners

➤ 1 cloth napkin,
20 x 20 in

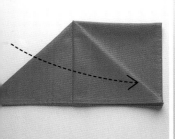

1 *Fold the napkin in half with the open end downward. Bring the bottom left corner, top layer only, over to the bottom right corner. Iron the triangle that is formed.*

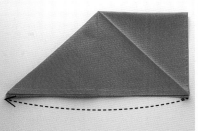

2 *Bring this corner back to where it was with the triangle now folded inward.*

3 *Bring the bottom right corner, top layer only, over to the bottom left corner and then fold over the point formed by the bottom layer. Iron and stand up the four-pointed napkin.*

13

Boat

➤ **1 cloth napkin, 20 x 20 in**

1 *Fold the napkin into quarters to form a square. Position it so that the four free corners are at the bottom left. Fold the bottom right corner up to the top left corner to form a triangle.*

2 *Fold the left side over (as shown in the photo) iron and unfold. Turn napkin over and fold and iron the same crease, but folded in the opposite direction. This time, do not unfold it. As in the photo, you now have two overlapping triangles, one smaller and one larger.*

3 *At its shorter end, turn the smaller triangle inside out so that one side of the triangle (four layers of the napkin) is o each side of the larger triangle Then stand it up.*

14

Advanced | Fancy

Flower Bud

➤ **1 cloth napkin, 20 x 20 in**

1 *Fold the napkin into quarters to form a square. Position it so that the four free corners are at the bottom.*

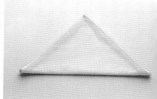

2 *Fold the bottom corner up to the top corner to form a triangle.*

3 *Fold in the sides of the triangle to meet in the center and iron well.*

4 *Fold the bottom points back and under so that they lie beneath the rest of the napkin.*

5 *Lift up the napkin and fold back the sides. Hold by the narrower end and iron.*

6 *Pull the layers of cloth up a little so they resemble the petals on a flower bud.*

15

Easy

Silverware Pocket

➤ 1 cloth napkin,
   16 x 16 in

1 Fold the top edge of the napkin down about 2¾ in. Then fold the bottom edge of this flap upward so it meets the top.

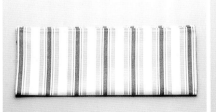

2 Turn the napkin over and fold the bottom edge up so it is flush with the top edge.

3 Fold the left and right ends toward the center so the napkin is folded into thirds and tuck one side into the other.

Easy
Cone

➤ 1 cloth napkin, 16 x 16 in

➤ For the filling:
   5 bread or pretzel rings
   1 candied lotus root
   2 cashew cookies
   Red melon seeds

1 Fold the left side of the napkin over the right.

2 Fold the top left corner down to the middle so you have a square and a triangle.

3 Fold the square upward and lay it on top of the triangle.

4 Turn the napkin over, from left to right like a page in a book.

5 Fold the back triangle down over the front and secure with a straight pin. The opening of the cone is on the left.

6 Fill the cone with bread rings, lotus root, cashew cookies, and melon seeds.

17

Classic | Festive

Bishop's Hat

➤ 1 cloth napkin, 20 x 20 in

1 *Fold the napkin into quarters to form a square. Position it so that the four free corners are at the bottom.*

2 *Fold the top layer up to the top corner.*

3 *Fold this top layer into accordion pleats about ³/₈ in wide.*

4 *Iron, turn the napkin over, and rotate ¼ turn.*

5 *Fold the bottom corner up to the top corner, fanning out the accordion pleats.*

6 *Pick up the napkin in both hands. Bring the two ends together and tuck them into one another so they are secured.*

Classic | Festive

Pointed Hat

➤ 1 cloth napkin, 20 x 20 in
  2 chopsticks

1 *Fold the left side of the napkin over the right. Fold down the two corners (as shown in the photo) so they meet at the center.*

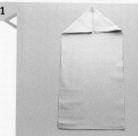

2 *Now fold down the point you formed and iron.*

3 *Turn the napkin over and again fold down the two top corners so they meet in the center and iron well.*

4 *Start at the bottom of the napkin, making accordion pleats ³/₄ in wide and iron. Stand the pointed hat upright and insert the chopsticks.*

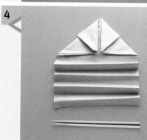

Fan

➤ 1 cloth napkin, 20 x 20 in

1 *Fold the napkin into a rectangle so that the narrow edges are at the top and bottom. Start at the bottom, making accordion pleats ³/₄ in wide until you reach the halfway point. Iron well.*

2 *Turn the napkin over with the accordion pleats underneath and rotate ¹/₄ turn.*

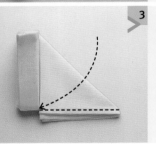

3 *Fold the napkin in half by bringing the bottom edge up to the top with the pleats on the outside. Fold the top right corner diagonally down to the folded base of the pleats and tuck the edge underneath.*

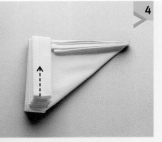

4 *Fold over the last free corner to form a triangle and iron well (photo shows back side). Stand the fan upright.*

Easy

Diamond in the Square

> 1 cloth napkin, 20 x 20 in

1 piece dried seaweed, $2\frac{1}{2}$ x $2\frac{1}{2}$ in

Japanese paper, $\frac{3}{4}$ x $1\frac{3}{4}$ in

1 pretty stone

Dried lychees (litchi nuts)

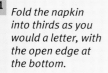

1 Fold the napkin into thirds as you would a letter, with the open edge at the bottom.

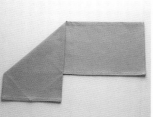

2 Fold down the top left corner to the center line and iron well. Turn the napkin over for step 3.

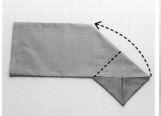

3 A small rectangle should be visible below right end of napkin. Fold up right and left corners of rectangle so they meet at center, fold up the end diagonally (shown), forming a diamond at right end.

3 Tuck the left end of the rectangle underneath to form the square.

21

Easy | Fancy

Elegant Silverware Pocket

➤ 1 cloth napkin, 20 x 20 in

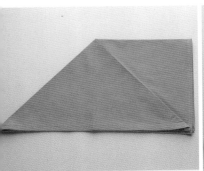

1 *Fold the napkin in half with the open end downward. Bring the bottom left corner, top layer only, over to the bottom right corner to form a triangle.*

2 *Turn over and again, bringing the bottom left corner, top layer only, over to the bottom right corner to form one large triangle. Iron well.*

3 *Fold in the ends from both sides in alternating layers and tuck them in to secure.*

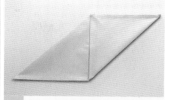

Fancy

Bird's Beak

➤ **1 cloth napkin, 20 x 20 in**

1 *Fold the napkin into a rectangle with the open side at the bottom.*

2 *Fold the top left corner down to the bottom edge and lower right corner up to the top edge.*

3 *Turn the napkin over and position it so that the top right corner is now at the bottom left. Fold the top half down over the bottom.*

4 *A small triangle should be visible at the top left.*

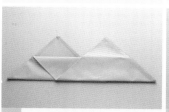

5 *Reach under the napkin and untuck the small triangle on the right. You now have two larger overlapping triangles.*

6 *Fold over the left corner of the left triangle as shown, tucking it into the right-hand triangle. Turn the napkin over and again tuck the left corner inside the triangle on the right.*

23

Artichoke

➤ 1 cloth napkin, 20 x 20 in
1 band, 2 x 6 in (any
desired paper or fabric)

1 *Begin with an open napkin, folding the top edge down about 4³/₄ in and folding the bottom edge up about 6¹/₄ in.*

2 *Start from the left, folding into accordion pleats. Iron very carefully to make sharp creases.*

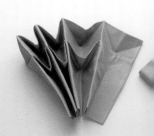

3 *Hold the napkin in your hand, first fold down the inner angles of the lower layer and then fold down the inner angles of the top layer. Secure the end with the band.*

Easy

Egg Cozy

➤ 1 cloth napkin, 20 x 20 in
1 colorful straight pin
1 decorative egg (optional)

Along the bottom edge, fold the napkin into three horizontal accordion pleats so that the edge of each pleat is visible above the pleat below it.

Turn the napkin over. Fold into thirds, first folding the left side toward the center and then the right. Tuck the ends into one another and iron well so that they hold.

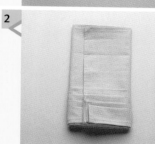

Fold down the top edge about 4 in.

Turn the napkin over and fold down the top edge about 2 in so the folds on the front and back are even, and secure with the straight pin. Plop the egg cozy onto the plate, or for a fun surprise, place a decorative egg underneath the napkin.

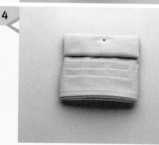

25

Quick and Easy Napkin Designs

A fancy design can turn even simple napkins into real eye-catchers, and with a little decorative touch, make pretty napkins into something truly beautiful. It takes very little time and costs almost nothing. You can also choose materials that hint at the meal to come, or use small objects from around the house for celebrating special seasons or occasions.

Easy

Gift-Wrapped Package

- 1 small gift

  1 box, approximately 4 x 4 x 1¼ in

  1 napkin, 16 x 16 in

  Orange felt, 3 x 14 in

  1 yd narrow yellow ribbon

  Pink felt, 2½ x 2½ in

  Glue

  1 bird Christmas ornament

  1 plastic flower

1 Place the gift in the box and seal it. Wrap the box in the napkin.

2 Wrap the orange felt band around the box. Encircle several times with the yellow ribbon and tie.

3 Glue the pink felt square in the center on top. Attach the bird to the flower and glue both onto the felt square.

Asian | Easy

Edible Charms

➤ Gray fabric, 6 x 10 in
1 napkin, 20 x 20 in
Needle and thread
2 slices candied lotus root
1 stick cinnamon
1 small bread ring
16 in string
1 piece dried seaweed, 2 x 2 in
1 colorful straight pin

1 | Fold the gray cloth into a 2 x 10 in strip. Iron the cloth flat.

2 | Fold the napkin into a square and position it with the four free corners at the bottom left. Fold the left side partway toward the center and lay the right side on top of it. Wrap the gray fabric around it as a band and sew it together at the back with several stitches.

3 | Thread the lotus root slices, cinnamon stick, and bread ring onto the string and tie.

4 | Place the seaweed on the band. Drape the string with the edible charms over it and attach with the straight pin.

Easy

Stone Charms

➤ 1 napkin, 20 x 20 in
Light-blue fabric, 4 in x 2 ft
Glue
1 stone with a hole
4 flat round beads
1 aluminum number
About 1 yd nylon thread (0.3 mm diameter)
1 round paper clip
3 dried plums
20 red melon seeds

1 | Fold the napkin in half. Then fold it into thirds by first folding in the left side and then the right, and turn the napkin over.

2 | Fold in the two long edges of the blue fabric to form a band 2 in wide and 2 ft long. Iron the fabric flat.

3 | Wrap the fabric strip lengthwise around the napkin as a band and glue it together at the back.

4 | String the stone, beads, and aluminum number onto a piece of nylon thread and tie. String the plums and melon seeds onto another piece of nylon thread and tie.

5 | Attach both strings to the paper clip and clip to the band.

TIP

To fasten the aluminum number more securely, you can also glue it to the top bead.

Photo left: **Napkin with Edible Charms**   *Photo right:* **Napkin with Stone Charms** ➤

Easy

Cross and Flower

➤ 1 napkin, 20 x 20 in
Red felt, $5^1/_2$ x $5^1/_2$ in
Glue
Light-red felt, $2^3/_8$ x $2^3/_8$ in
Pink felt, $2^3/_8$ x $2^3/_8$ in
Orange felt, $3^1/_4$ x $3^1/_4$ in
Yellow felt, $3^1/_4$ x $3^1/_4$ in
Needle and thread

1 | Fold the napkin into a 10 x 10 in square.

2 | Cut the red felt into a cross, and glue or sew it onto the center of the napkin.

3 | Cut out two larger flower petals and two smaller flower petals, one from each of the four different colored felts.

4 | Stack the smaller petals on top of one another. Hold them together at the base and pull them apart slightly at the top. Place the two larger petals around the smaller petals and sew the flower together.

5 | Sew the flower to the cross

with several stitches.

Easy

Decorated Border

➤ Pink, purple, and red felt scraps, about $1^3/_8$ x 2 in
5 pink tassels
5 red tassels
1 napkin, 20 x 20 in
Needle and thread
20 pink, red, and orange sequins
20 pink, red, and orange glass beads
5 pink flower sequins or spangles

1 | Cut the felt scraps into rectangles of varying sizes.

2 | Arrange the felt rectangles and tassels in alternating order and colors along the underside of the napkin border and sew on.

3 | Decoratively distribute sequins and beads over the napkin and sew them in place.

4 | Sew the flower sequins or spangles along the napkin border.

5 | Fold the napkin so as to highlight the decorated border.

TIP

After folding the napkin, you can also choose to decorate only the visible side with sequins and beads. Naturally, this won't require as many materials.

Photo top: **Napkin with Cross and Flower**   Photo bottom: **Decorated Border Napkin** ➤

Easy
Paper Collage

➤ Scraps of paper, small pictures, and clippings (form a mini-collage, 2 x 2 in)

Glue

Needle and thread

1 napkin, 16 x 16 in

1 metal letter

1 button

1 piece silver paper, ³⁄₄ x ³⁄₄ in

1 small plastic doll or cherub

1 piece translucent vellum paper, 1¹⁄₂ x 1¹⁄₂ in

Waterproof pen

1 | Using the paper scraps, pictures, and clippings, glue together a small collage that fits onto the napkin.

2 | Sew the collage to the folded napkin with several stitches.

3 | Sew the metal letter (for example, the first letter of the guest's name) and the plastic doll or cherub to the napkin.

4 | Glue the button to the silver paper, and sew both to the napkin.

5 | Write text on the vellum paper (for example, the menu) and sew it to the napkin.

Easy
Mirrors

➤ Gray felt, 4 x 8 in

10 small mirrors (1 in diameter)

Glue

1 napkin, 20 x 20 in

Needle and gray thread

10 transparent glass beads

1 | Cut the felt into 1³⁄₈ x 1¹⁄₂ in ovals. Cut ⁵⁄₈ x 1 in ovals out of the centers of these larger ovals to form oval felt rings.

2 | Glue the felt rings to the mirrors as frames. Distribute over the napkin and attach each one with several stitches.

3 | Decoratively arrange the glass beads in the spaces between and sew them in place.

TIP

To make the felt rings as nice as possible, draw them on the felt before cutting them out with the scissors!

Photo left: **Napkin with Mirrors**   *Photo right:* **Napkin with Paper Collage** ➤

Easy

Paper Fringe

- Double-sided transparent adhesive tape, ⅜ x 20 in
  1 napkin, 20 x 20 in
  Scraps of colored paper
  Multicolored narrow ribbons
  20 in strip of orange fringe

1 | Affix double-sided adhesive tape onto the back of the napkin along the edge so it is sticky from both sides.

2 | Cut the paper scraps into ¾ x 1½ in pieces. Alternating the colors, stick these rectangles onto the adhesive tape, forming a colorful paper fringe along the border. Leave a few gaps for slightly longer pieces of colored ribbon.

3 | Cut the ribbons into 2¾ in pieces and attach them between the paper pieces.

4 | Affix the orange fringe along the top front edge of the napkin.

TIP

You can make the paper fringe napkin using either paper or cloth napkins. The fringed border can easily be removed from cloth napkins after the party.

Fast

Tear-Off

- 20 paper napkins of different colors
  1 hole punch
  1 yd string

1 | Fold each paper napkin in half lengthwise.

2 | At the narrow end, punch a hole in the middle of the napkins, positioning the hole as close to the edge as possible so it will be easy to tear off the napkins later on.

3 | After punching the holes, arrange the napkins on the string in a colorful fan and tie the string long enough so you can easily hang up your tear-off bundle.

TIPS

Another idea is to fold the paper napkins diagonally and punch a hole in one corner. You can also use these tear-off napkins to express certain themes. For example, string together green, white, and orange napkins for a Mexican fiesta; red, pink, and white for Valentine's Day; or red, white, and blue for a patriotic theme.

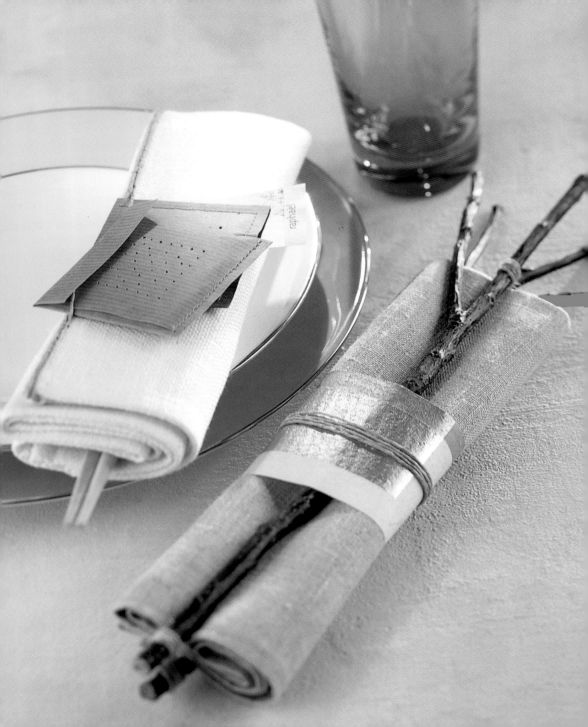

Easy
Spice Sachets

MAKES 1 SACHET

- Brown wrapping paper,
  3 x 7 in
  Needle and thread
  Dried spices
  (e.g., ginger, aniseed,
  coriander seeds, cloves)
  20 in string
  Glue
  1 napkin, 20 x 20 in
  1 paper scrap,
  $2\frac{3}{8}$ x $2\frac{3}{8}$ in
  Marker

1 | Fold the brown wrapping paper twice in order to form a 7 x $2\frac{3}{8}$ in rectangle.

2 | Sew together along the two longer edges and one of the narrower edges.

3 | At the open fourth edge fold down a $\frac{3}{4}$ in wide strip to resemble the flap on an envelope.

4 | Use the sewing needle to pierce the envelope with many tiny holes so the scent of the spices can escape.

5 | For each napkin, fill two envelopes with spices and pass a string under the flaps.

6 | Glue the flaps closed and sew both ends of the string to the napkin with several stitches to secure the spice sachets.

7 | Write the guest's name on the scrap of paper and insert it between the sachets.

TIP Naturally, you can also use paper envelopes of the appropriate size.

Vary the spice mixture to match your taste, the occasion, or the menu.

Fast
Twigs

- 1 napkin, 20 x 20 in
  Gift wrap, 2 x 8 in
  Glue
  20 in string
  2 twigs (1 ft long,
  about $\frac{3}{8}$ in diameter)

1 | Fold the napkin in half and roll up, starting from the narrow end.

2 | Wrap gift paper around the napkin and glue it together at the back.

3 | Insert one twig between the napkin and band in the front, and one twig in the back.

4 | Wrap the string around the band.

5 | Wrap the string around both ends of the twigs and tie them together.

TIP Use twigs with blossoms and leaves typical of the season.

Nostalgic
Victorian Scrap Collage

➤ 1 napkin, 20 x 20 in
1 Victorian scrap, 3 x 6 in
Needle and thread
3 small plastic leaves
15 green sequins
15 green glass beads

1 | Fold the napkin in thirds, then into a square, and then into a rectangle.

2 | Sew the Victorian scrap onto the napkin with several stitches.

3 | Insert the stem ends of the plastic leaves under the edges of the Victorian scrap and sew them in place.

4 | Decoratively arrange the sequins and glass beads on the napkin and sew them in place.

TIP Instead of Victorian scraps, have pictures of flowers color copied at your local copy shop, cut them out, and sew or glue them onto the napkin.

Easy
Napkin Line

➤ 1 yd string
1 napkin, 20 x 20 in
Translucent vellum paper, $3^{1}/_{2}$ x $9^{3}/_{4}$ in
Paint marker (white)
20 dried chile peppers
Sewing needle
20 in nylon thread
Gift wrap, $6^{1}/_{4}$ x 8 in
1 clothespin

1 | Tie a string to the back of a chair so the string looks like it sags slightly.

2 | Fold the napkin in half lengthwise and hang it from the string by the narrow end.

3 | Use the paint marker to write on the vellum paper (for example, the menu).

4 | String the chile peppers onto the nylon thread.

5 | Place the vellum paper on the gift paper. Use the clothespin to attach the papers and the napkin to the string.

6 | Drape the chile peppers over the napkin.

SALAT
MIT
WALNUSS
VINAIGRETTE

*

FISCH
TERRINE

*

GRANAT
APFEL
SUPPE

*

Easy
Paper Pattern I

➤ 1 napkin, 20 x 20 in
   Parchment paper in 3
   shades of blue,
   3 x 3 in each
   Needle and thread
   20 in orange and 20 in
   red ribbon
   1 piece of gold paper,
   $1^1/_4$ x $1^1/_4$ in
   Glue

1 | Fold the napkin into thirds.

2 | Fold parchment paper
squares into quarters and
then fold in half diagonally,
forming triangles. Use a pair
of scissors to cut out little
patterns and shapes.

3 | Unfold parchment paper
and either smooth it out with
your hands or iron.

4 | Glue the parchment
squares together in a strip
and sew them onto the
center of the napkin with
several stitches.

5 | Wrap both ribbons
lengthwise around the
napkin and tie.

6 | Glue the gold paper over
the ribbons at the middle.

Easy
Paper Pattern II

➤ Translucent vellum paper,
   $6^3/_4$ x $12^1/_2$ in
   1 light-blue, 1 light-green,
   and 1 dark-blue paper
   napkin
   Artificial grass, 6 x $7^1/_2$ in
   Eyelet pliers
   1 silver eyelet
   1 sequin flower
   Glue
   Waterproof pen
   (black or dark color)
   1 bundle green raffia

1 | Start from a narrow end,
folding the vellum paper
upward $4^1/_4$ in and glue the
two sides together to form
a pocket.

2 | Cut the light-blue napkin
into a $4^3/_4$ x $4^3/_4$ in square.

3 | Cut the green napkin into
a $4^1/_4$ x $4^1/_4$ in square.

4 | Cut the dark-blue napkin
into a $3^1/_4$ x 4 in square.

5 | Stack the napkins on top
of one another and place at
one end of the artificial grass.
Punch a hole through them
all with the eyelet pliers and
set the eyelet. Glue the flower
sequin onto the eyelet.

6 | Place this bundle inside
the vellum paper pocket.

7 | Write on the paper pocket
with the waterproof pen.

8 | Drape with the green raffia
inside as decoration.

TIP

You can also use
readymade transparent
envelopes, (available
in various colors).
You can also print text
onto these envelopes,
if you have a home
printer available.

Photo top: **Paper Pattern I Napkin**   *Photo bottom:* **Paper Pattern II Napkin**

pure morning

Radicchiosalat
mit Blütenessig

Gemüseragout
mit rotem Pfeffer

Orangenkuchen
in Sirup

menu
cherry peppers sottolio
red snapper mit chilisauce
grapefruittarte
beerensorbet

Easy
Menu in a Box

➤ 1 box, 4³⁄₄ x 4³⁄₄ x 2 in
(from a store)
Light-blue tempera paint
Paintbrush
A pretty, colorful picture
Silver paper, 3¹⁄₄ x 4 in
Glue
Black pen
White translucent vellum
paper, 2 x 8 in
Light-blue translucent
vellum paper, 3¹⁄₄ x 8 in
1 napkin, 20 in x 20 in
Needle and thread

1 | Paint the box with
light-blue tempera paint
and let dry.

2 | Cut out the picture and
glue it onto the silver paper.

3 | Glue the silver paper
onto the painted box.

4 | Write the menu on the
white translucent vellum
paper with the black pen.

5 | Glue the white translucent
vellum paper onto the center
of the light-blue translucent
vellum paper.

6 | Fold the napkin so that it
fits inside the box. Sew the
menu to the napkin with
one stitch on each side.

Easy
Menu Attached

➤ 1 napkin, 20 x 20 in
2 strips of translucent
vellum paper, each
2 x 11³⁄₄ in
Waterproof pen
1 pretty, colorful picture
Needle and thread
Eyelet pliers
2 silver eyelets
2 incense sticks

1 | Fold the napkin in half
and then into thirds, forming
a narrow rectangle.

2 | Write the menu on one
piece of vellum paper.

3 | Cut out the picture and
sew it onto the napkin with
several stitches.

4 | Position the blank piece of
vellum paper lengthwise
under the napkin and place
the menu on top of it.

5 | Punch holes in both
ends of the paper strips
with the eyelet pliers, and
set the eyelets.

6 | Insert the incense sticks
under the paper band.

Fancy Napkin Packaging

Give your napkins a highly sophisticated look by packaging them with simple but effective media. Even if you aren't very "artsy," you can still design impressive napkins that highlight the character of your menu before you've served the first course.

Easy

String of Beads

➤ 1 napkin, 20 x 20 in

14 unglazed clay beads ($1/2$ in diameter)

7 flat mother-of-pearl beads ($3/4$ in diameter)

1 flat mother-of-pearl bead ($1 1/4$ in diameter)

2 ft string

Sprig of 6 small chile peppers

1 *Roll up the napkin. String the beads so that two clay beads alternate with each small mother-of-pearl bead.*

2 *String the large mother-of-pearl bead at the end and tie off the string.*

3 *Wrap the string of beads around the center of the napkin and insert the chile pepper sprig under the string.*

Easy
Edible Band

➤ 8 in each of orange, red, and pink fringe
Red felt, 1¾ x 8 in
Needle and red thread
1 napkin, 20 x 20 in
1 oz dried red lychees
1 ft nylon thread
1 silver bead
1 orange rice cracker

1 | Sew the fringe strips to the edge of the red felt.

2 | Fold the napkin into a narrow rectangle, wrap the red felt around the napkin, and sew it together at the back with several stitches.

3 | String the lychees onto the nylon thread with the silver bead in the center.

4 | Tie off the string of lychees and wrap it around the felt band.

5 | Insert the orange rice cracker beneath the felt band.

Fast
Flower and Herb Napkin Ring

➤ 1 napkin, 20 x 20 in
Turquoise felt, 1½ x 8 in
Needle and thread
20 in silver wire (1 mm diameter)
1 paper flower
Fresh flowers and sprigs of herbs (optional)

1 | Fold the napkin in half and roll it up tightly.

2 | Wrap the felt strip around the napkin and sew it together at the back with several stitches.

3 | Wrap the silver wire several times around the ring and tie.

4 | Insert the paper flower, and fresh herbs and flowers, if using between the ring and the napkin.

TIP
You can also use plastic flowers instead of fresh ones, since they will last longer.

Photo left: **Edible Band**   *Photo top:* **Flower and Herb Napkin Ring** ➤

Easy

Postcard Pocket

- 2 postcards
  Glue
  Eyelet pliers
  2 silver eyelets
  1 napkin, 20 x 20 in

1 | Have the postcards color copied and enlarged to 5½ x 7½ in at your local copy shop.

2 | Fold back ⅜ in along the bottom edge (long or short end, depending on the orientation of the pictures) of each enlargement.

3 | Place the folded edges on top of one another and glue them together to form a pocket with a printed picture visible on each side.

4 | Stand the pocket upright, pinch the two pictures together, and punch a hole in the middle on each end. Place the silver eyelets together and squeeze.

5 | Stand up the postcard pocket and insert a napkin that has been folded to fit.

Inexpensive

Twig Napkin Ring

- 1 napkin, 20 x 20 in
  60 thin, dried twigs, about 2¾ in long
  1 flower wire

1 | Fold the napkin into quarters and fold this square into thirds.

2 | Wrap the flower wire several times around the center of the first twig.

3 | Place the second twig next to the first and wrap the wire around it once. Do the same with all the remaining twigs, forming a strip of twigs.

4 | Bend this strip into a ring and fasten it with flower wire.

5 | Place the napkin inside the twig napkin ring.

Photo top: **Postcard Pocket** *Photo bottom:* **Twig Napkin Ring**

Easy
Felt Pocket

➤ Gray-brown felt,
5 x 17 in
Needle and thread
Silver-white Japanese
paper, 1³⁄₄ x 2 in
Glue
1 flower-shaped
silver bead
1 green mother-of-
pearl bead
Eyelet pliers
1 silver eyelet
20 in narrow green
elastic band
4 small red beads
on threads

1 | Fold the felt strip lengthwise leaving about 6 in uncovered at one end. Sew together the two sides.

2 | Glue the Japanese paper at the top edge of the pocket in the center. Sew the flower-shaped silver bead and mother-of-pearl bead to the center of the Japanese paper.

3 | Punch a hole in the center of the back flap and set the eyelet. Insert the elastic band through the eyelet and tie.

4 | Close the pocket and wrap the elastic band around it.

5 | Tie the red beads on threads to the flower-shaped silver bead.

Easy
Felt Croissant Band

➤ Black felt, 6¹⁄₄ x 11³⁄₄ in
Gray-brown felt,
5¹⁄₂ x 11 in
Glue
1 silver eyelet
Eyelet pliers
20 in twine
1 natural-colored linen
napkin, 20 x 20 in
1 dark incense stick
2 guinea fowl feathers
(from art supply stores
or hobby shops)

1 | Cut the black felt into a triangle 11³⁄₄ in high and 6¹⁄₄ in wide at the base. Cut the gray-brown felt into a triangle 11 in high and 5¹⁄₂ in wide at the base.

2 | Glue the smaller felt triangle onto the center of the larger triangle so that a ³⁄₈ in strip of the black felt is visible on either side of the gray-brown triangle.

3 | Using the eyelet pliers, set the silver eyelet at the narrow end of the felt triangle. Pass the twine through the eyelet and tie.

4 | Fold the napkin in half and roll it up. Starting with the wide end, roll the felt triangle around the center of the napkin as a band, wrap the string around it, and tie.

5 | Decorate the band with the incense stick and feathers.

Easy

Paper Envelope

- ➤ 2 pieces of blue-gray photographic cardboard, 6¼ x 6¼ in

   Needle and light-blue thread

   1 aluminum number

   Glue

   1 silver bead

   1 napkin, 20 x 20 in

1 | Place one square of photo cardboard on top of the other and sew the two squares together on three sides with large stitches to form a pocket-like envelope.

2 | Apply a little glue to the aluminum number and glue it to the envelope.

3 | Glue the silver bead (flat or flower-shaped as in the photo) beside the number.

4 | Fold the napkin so it fits inside the envelope and insert it.

TIPS

A blue-gray paper envelope has a more sophisticated look while other colors, such as neon colors, give the table setting a more colorful appearance. Instead of these aluminum numbers, you can also create numbers out of aluminum foil.

Fast

Aluminum Foil Sculpture

- ➤ 1 napkin, 20 x 20 in

   20 in silver wire

   5 strips of aluminum foil, each 4 in wide

   1 plastic flower with stem

1 | Fold the napkin in half and roll it up tightly.

2 | Wrap the silver wire several times around the napkin to form a ring. Leave one end of the wire extended upwards—this is where you will attach the aluminum foil sculpture.

3 | Twist each strip of aluminum foil to form cord-like objects.

4 | Twist the "foil cords" into curving, ornamental shapes.

5 | Twist the five cords together at one end and attach them to the napkin ring with the silver wire.

6 | Insert the plastic flower between the ring and the napkin.

Easy

Plastic Asian Pocket

➤ 1 food pkg from an Asian store
Needle and thread
2 chopsticks
1 napkin, 20 x 20 in

1 | At a copy store, have two copies made of the food package, enlarged to at least 4 x 11 in.

2 | Cut one copy into a 4 x 7 in rectangle.

3 | Have the two copies laminated separately and cut them out.

4 | Place the smaller laminated copy on top of the larger one and align the bottom edges. Using the needle and thread, sew the edges together along the two sides and at the bottom with large stitches.

5 | Insert the chopsticks and the folded napkin.

Easy

Typographic French Fry Cone

➤ 1 quarter-circle of paper printed with text, straight edges about 10 in long
Glue
1 quarter-circle of black and white gift paper, straight edges about 10 in long
Hole punch
20 in elastic string
1 napkin, 20 x 20 in

1 | At a local copy store, have the paper with text copied onto transparency paper, such as the type used with overhead projectors.

2 | Cut the film into a quarter-circle with 10 in sides and twist into a cone. Glue the cone together at the seam.

3 | Cut the gift wrap into a quarter circle with 10 in sides as well, twist into a cone, and glue together.

4 | Place the black-and-white gift paper cone inside the transparent typewritten plastic cone.

5 | At the upper edges of the cone, punch holes through both cones and attach the elastic string.

6 | Fill the cone with the napkin and close it with the elastic string.

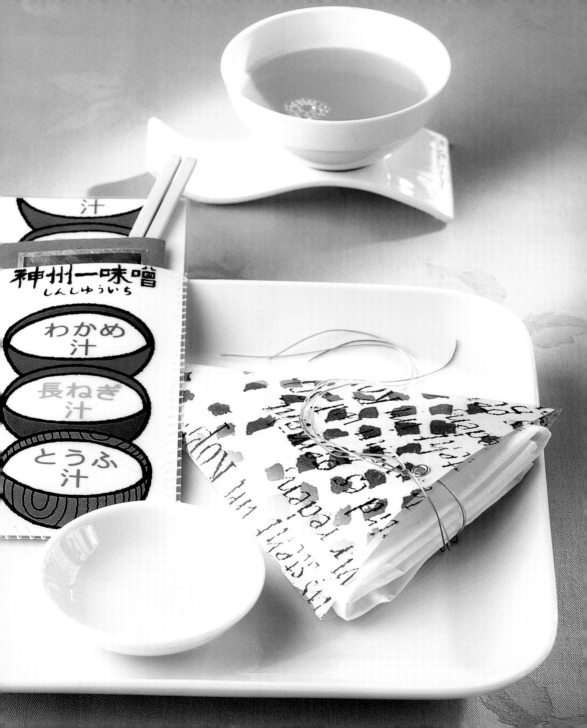

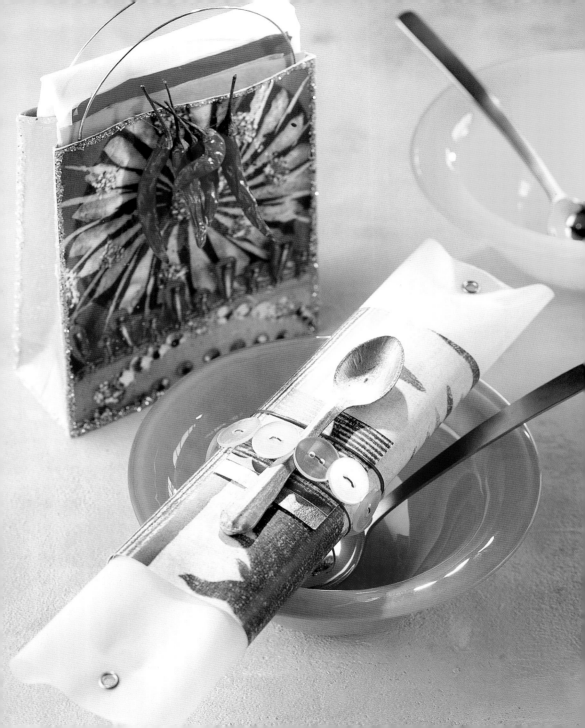

Easy

Paper Bag with Handle

➤ Brown paper bag, 5 x 6$\frac{1}{4}$ in

Patterned gift paper, about 8 x 16 in

Glue

Silver glitter

2 pieces of silver wire, each 10 in

4 strips of tissue paper, 4$\frac{1}{4}$ x 16 in, in the following colors: light-pink, dark-pink, white, and orange

1 napkin, 20 x 20 in

6 small red chile peppers

Needle and thread

1 | Glue the patterned gift paper to the paper bag.

2 | Apply the glue around the edges of the gift paper, and sprinkle with silver glitter.

3 | Bend both pieces of the silver wire into half circles.

4 | Glue the wires to the inside of the paper bag to form handles.

5 | Once the glue has dried, arrange the tissue paper strips and napkin inside the bag.

6 | String the chile peppers together with needle and thread and attach them to the handles, resembles a small garland (see photo).

Button Band

➤ 1 napkin, 20 x 20 in

Translucent vellum paper, 8 x 11$\frac{3}{4}$ in

Glue

Gift wrap, 6$\frac{3}{4}$ x 8 in

10 buttons (about $\frac{3}{4}$ in diameter)

20 in fine thread

2 eyelets

Eyelet pliers

1 spoon

1 | Fold the napkin in half and roll it up.

2 | Wrap the vellum paper around the napkin and glue it together at the back so that it extends about one inch beyond the napkin at both ends.

3 | Wrap the gift paper around the vellum paper and glue it together at the back.

4 | String the buttons on the thread. Wrap the string of buttons around the napkin and tie.

5 | Close up the vellum paper at both ends with the eyelets.

6 | Insert the spoon under the button band.

Easy
Colorful Box

- ➤ Box, 5 x 5 x 1¼ in (from a craft store or use old stationery boxes)
  Tempera paint
  Paintbrush
  1 napkin, 16 x 16 in
  1 plastic measuring tape
  1 piece of tissue paper, 5 x 16 in

1 | Using a paintbrush and tempera paint, paint the box whatever color you choose and let dry.

2 | Fold the napkin into a square so that it fits perfectly inside the box and wrap the measuring tape around it.

3 | Line the box with the tissue paper, and place the napkin and measuring tape on top.

TIP You can also glue the rose to the Japanese paper.

Easy
Felt Pouch with Fringe and Rose

- ➤ Red felt, 8 x 12½ in
  Needle and red thread
  8 in each of orange, red, and pink fringe
  Orange-gold Japanese paper, 1¾ x 3⅜ in
  Glue
  1 silk rose
  2 red beads
  1 napkin, 20 x 20 in

1 | Fold the felt 4¾ in up from the bottom. Sew the two sides together with red thread.

2 | Sew the strips of fringe to the bottom, closed end. Arrange them so they overlap one another slightly.

3 | Glue the Japanese paper at the top edge of the pouch in the center and sew the rose to the Japanese paper with several stitches.

4 | Sew the red beads to the bottom two corners of the Japanese paper.

5 | Fold the napkin and place it in the pouch.

Photo top: Colorful Box   *Photo bottom:* **Felt Pouch with Fringe and Rose** ➤

Using this index
To make it easier for you
to find instructions that
use specific materials, this
index lists favorite materials
(such as felt or eyelets) in
bold type, followed by the
corresponding instructions.

ABBREVIATIONS
ft = feet
in = inch
mm = millimeter
pkg = package
yd = yard

The Author

Caroline Hofman studied graphic design and now freelances, mainly for magazine publishers in Europe. Her favorite areas are styling, food, packaging, and creative productions. It is with great joy that this Dutch native and her 9-year-old son, Raphael, immerse themselves in the imaginative realm of children's art to create magical productions.

The Photographers

Manfred Jahreiß works as an independent photographer. Together with his team, he operates two photography studios in Europe. He comes from an area of Germany known for fabulous tableware manufacturers, and has created a name for himself in this industry. As the head photographer in his Munich studio, **Eva Wunderlich** has created an entire gallery of photographs for German book publishers, using atmospheric and multifaceted imagery. Jahreiß and Wunderlich would like to thank the following companies for their kind support: Dibbern, Rosenthal AG, SKV-Arzberg, Villeroy and Boch AG.

Photo Credits

Cover photo: Jörn Rynio
All others: Studio Jahreiß

Published originally under the title Servietten falten: kleine Kniffe—große Wirkung © 2003 Gräfe und Unzer Verlag GmbH, Munich. English translation for the U.S. market © 2004, Silverback Books, Inc.

Program director: Doris Birk
Managing editor: Lisa M. Tooker, Birgit Rademacker
Translator: Christie Tam
Editor: Ann Beman, Stefanie Poziombka,
Reader: Margit Proebst
Layout, typography and cover design: Independent Medien Design, Munich
Typesetting: Patty Holden, Verlagssatz Lingner
Production: Patty Holden, Helmut Giersberg

Printed in China

ISBN 1-930603-44-4

Enjoy Other Quick & Easy Books

Coffee and Espresso

Tanja Dusy

Christmas Cookies

1 Pan— 50 Muffins

Fast Italian

Margit Proebst

Andreas Fürtmayr

Sauces and Dips

Irresistible Fondue

Angelika Ilies

Cooking for Two

Cornelia Adam

Healthy Wok

Elisabeth Döpp
Christian Willrich
Björn Krönke

Great for light and satisfying meals

Antje Muliar

Grilling

Andreas Fürtmayr

Sushi

Classic ideas from Japan
and new fusion sushi
Home-made perfectly

Gina Greifenstein

1 Batter— 50 Cakes

Baking to your heart's content

Cooking in Clay

Healthy Recipes with Great Flavor

Erika Casparek-Türkkan

1 Noodle, 50 Sauces

Everyday Pasta • Old and New Italian Dishes
Noodle Geography • 10 Tips for Success

Chris Muliar

Cocktails for Drivers

100% Enjoyment

Antipasti and Tapas

Mediterranean Appetizers
Cornelia Schinharl

Soups

Classic to Contemporary

Sebastian Dickhaut

Claudia Schmidt

Raclette

New Recipes with Cheese-Primer and Party Dips

Cornelia Schinharl

Easy Vegetarian

Uncomplicated and sophisticated—
Vegetarian recipes for all seasons

Cornelia Adam

Garlic

dicated flavors with the taste
of the Mediterranean Region
(famous fine (delicate) international

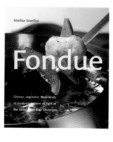

Marlisa Szwillus

Fondue

Cheese, vegetable, or all kinds
of meat—cook them all right at
the table, then their blessings

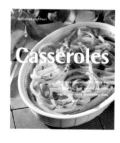

Sebastian Dickhaut

Casseroles

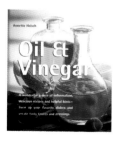

Annette Heisch

Oil & Vinegar

A wonderful source of information,
delicious recipes and helpful hints—
liven up your favorite dishes and
create tasty sauces and dressings

Cornelia Adam

Quiche

delicious, easy to make, with
vegetables, meat, poultry or
fish—ideas for all occasions

LOOK AROUND THE HOUSE

➤ All these instructions are meant to serve only as inspirations to search your house, open up drawers, and combine all sorts of fun and creative objects. Go wherever your mood takes you! You'll be surprised at what you'll find in your own home for creative napkin design.

Guaranteed Perfect Napkins

NAPKIN FOLDING— BE PREPARED I

➤ Ninety-percent of successful napkin folding is in the correct preparation of the cloth napkin.

➤ It's best to iron the napkins into their final shape several days in advance and press them between books.

WRITING ON NAPKINS

➤ Naturally, you can also write on the napkins directly. This is a quick and easy way to add an even more personal touch to your napkin creation. There are special markers for almost any material. For example, Crayola or Marvy fabric markers are great for cloth napkins. It's always best to ask for advice at the craft or art supply store where you make your purchase.

SEWING INSTEAD OF GLUEING

➤ Although working with glue is much faster than sewing materials together with several stitches, it's hard to wash out. If you want to be able to reuse your napkins, it would be worth your while to invest the little bit of extra time.